D0132499

Beautiful Bags

for the Crafty Fashionista

by Kara L. Laughlin

FashionCraft
Studio

WITHDRAWN

CAPSTONE PRESS
a capstone imprint

Snap Books are published by Capstone Press.
1710 Roe Crest Drive, North Mankato, Mankato, Minnesota 56003
www.capstonepub.com

Copyright © 2012 by Capstone Press, a Capstone imprint.
All rights reserved.
No part of this publication may be reproduced in whole or in part, or stored in a retrieval system,
or transmitted in any form or by any means, electronic, mechanical, photocopying, recording,
or otherwise, without written permission of the publisher.
For information regarding permission, write to Capstone Press,
1710 Roe Crest Drive, North Mankato, Minnesota 56003.

Books published by Capstone Press are manufactured with paper
containing at least 10 percent post-consumer waste.

Library of Congress Cataloging-in-Publication Data

Laughlin, Kara L.
Reusing bags for the crafty fashionista / by Kara L. Laughlin.
       p. cm. — (Snap books. Crafting green style)
Includes bibliographical references and index.
Summary: "Step-by-step instructions to create purses, baskets, and other bag crafts made from repurposed
materials"—Provided by publisher.
ISBN 978-1-4296-6550-6 (library binding)
1. Handbags—Juvenile literature. 2. Garbage. Waste. 3. Recycling—Juvenile literature. 4. Handicraft for girls—Juvenile literature.
I. Title. II. Series.

Editorial Credits
Mandy Robbins, editor
Heidi Thompson, designer
Marcie Spence, media researcher
Laura Manthe, production specialist

Photo Credits
All photos by Capstone Studio: Karon Dubke; Shutterstock: Lawren (cover, design element)

The author would like to thank Roxane Quimby for starting it all with Burt's Bees.

Table of C

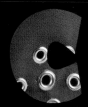

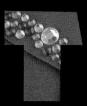

Happening Handbags

You can go anywhere in this world with a good haircut, the right shoes, and a great handbag. At least, that's what it says in the style magazines. The projects in this book will help you make sure you've always got the right bag for the occasion. Whether it's a school dance or lunch with your BFFs at the mall, your bag will help you stand out in the crowd.

Time for a Change

If you love updating and making your own bags, you can move on to designing and customizing. Use your skill to create cute accents, add interesting details, or give the bag a whole new look. The directions in this book are only ideas. You might not have the same bags, fabric, trim, or decorations as shown. Don't worry! Let your inner designer create one-of-a-kind bags your friends will envy!

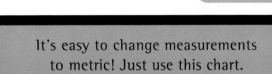

It's easy to change measurements to metric! Just use this chart.

To change	into	multiply by
inches	centimeters	2.54
inches	millimeters	25.4
feet	meters	.305
yards	meters	.914

envy—to want something owned by another

Fringe Benefits

Silly shaped silicone bands are fun for a while, but all trends end. If you're over the rainbow-on-your-arm look, use them to give a boring purse some funky fringe.

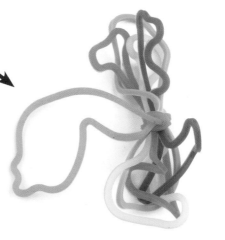

You Will Need:

silicone rubber bands
scissors
drawstring handbag

 **Step one:**
Set one silicone band horizontally on a table. Lay four silicone bands vertically across the single band.

 **Step two:**
Loop one end of the single band through the other. Pull the single band tight around the other bands.

 **Step three:**
Fold the four bands in half.

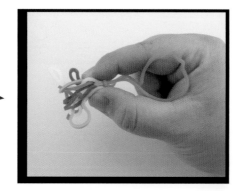

Step four:

Wrap and tie a new silicone band tightly around the top of the folded bundle. Cut the bottoms of the folded bands to make a tassel.

Step five:

Thread the single silicone band under the purse's drawstring. Pull the loop over the drawstring and push the tassel through. Pull tight.

Step six:

Continue adding fringe around the top of the bag.

 **Variation:**
- Make your accessories match by using the tassels as zipper pulls or keychains.

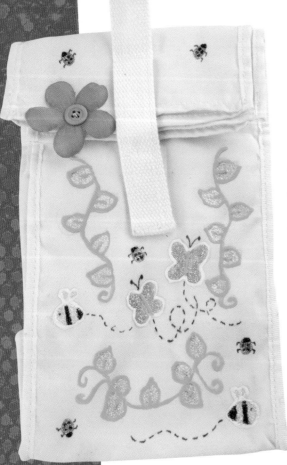

Garden Party

Give the term "going green" some color with this flashy reusable lunch bag. Your friends will be green with envy over this clever and colorful upgrade. Heads will turn when you bring your lunch to the table.

You Will Need:

scissors
fabric flower lei
fabric lunch bag
needle and thread
buttons
puffy paint pens
glitter glue

Step one:
Cut the lei and
unstring the flowers.

Step two:
Decide where you want to place
the flowers on the bag.

❋ Variations:
- Use a lei made from shells
  for a more natural look.
- Draw fish and ocean plants
  instead of bugs and stems.

Step three:
Sew flowers and buttons to bag. For sewing tips, go to page 16.

Step four:
Use puffy paint to draw stems and leaves up the front of the bag. Let dry.

Step five:
Use glitter glue to paint bugs, butterflies, and bees in between the stems and flowers. Let the glue dry before using.

Tip: Don't bring a lunch bag to school? Try this design on a messenger bag.

Sentimental Scrap

Don't let your bag get lost in a crowd! This craft will make it easier to find your bag at the gym or your luggage at the airport. Decoupage glue is a great way to hang onto sentimental items like ticket stubs, invitations, or photos.

You Will Need:

sandpaper

bag made with a firm
   material, such as leather,
   vinyl, or plastic

scissors

paper cutouts, such as ticket
   stubs, maps, or photographs

decoupage glue

foam paintbrush

craft glue

large rhinestones

 Step one:
Lightly sand the sides
of your purse.

 Step two:
Trim the paper cutouts into small
pieces, if necessary. Lay pieces
onto the purse to plan your pattern.

Tip: It may take up
to 12 coats of decoupage
glue to make the paper feel
completely smooth.

10

 ## Step three:

Use the foam paintbrush to coat the bag with decoupage glue.

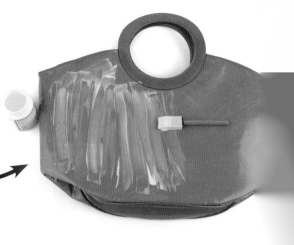

 ## Step four:

Coat the back of the paper cutout with decoupage glue. Press paper cutout onto purse. Use your fingers to flatten paper, if necessary. Let dry.

 ## Step five:

Apply a coat of decoupage glue over the top of the cutout. Let dry. Repeat until the purse is completely smooth.

 ## Step six:

Use craft glue to attach rhinestones to the purse.

decoupage—a liquid glue used in craft projects

sentimental—resulting from feelings rather than facts

Glittering Grommets

Grommets are both stylish and functional. They easily update the look of a tote bag. You can find them at craft, fabric, and hardware stores. Then use your new bag to carry clothes to a sleepover or your homework to class.

You Will Need:

fabric tote bag
1 or 2 packages of ⁵/₁₆"
    grommets with setter
pencil
scissors
hammer

Step one:

Plan your design on the bag. Mark the placement of the grommets with pencil.

✳ *Variation*:

- Use smaller grommets on a gift or party favor bag. Thread ribbon through the grommet holes. Then use the small bag to carry your sunglasses, cell phone, or makeup.

grommet—a ring that strengthens
   or protects an opening

Step two:
Use scissors to make small Xs through the bag at each mark.

Step three:
Cut out holes in the purse at each X.

Step four:
Use the hammer and the directions on the grommet package to set grommets through each hole.

Tip: If you prefer, you can hot glue the grommets onto the bag, rather than using the grommet setter.

Crunchy **Cosmetics**

Makeup is great to have on hand, but it can leave your cosmetics bag a mess. This bag is easy to clean and easy to replace! Keep your accessories close for any emergency touch-ups.

You Will Need:

scissors

ruler

clean breakfast cereal bag

plastic netting

stapler

flat decorations like metal confetti, sequins, and pictures

zipper

duct tape

Step one:

Cut the bottom 6 inches off the cereal bag. Discard the top.

Step two:

Cut a piece of netting the same width as the cereal bag and twice as long.

Tip: Going green? Use old produce bags instead of netting.

Step three:

Wrap the netting completely around the cereal bag. Staple the cut ends of the netting to the side of the bag.

Step four:

Staple the bottom edge of the bag. Leave the top of the bag open.

Step five:

Tuck decorations between the net and the cereal bag.

Step six:

Unzip the zipper. Cut to the same width of the bag.

Step seven:

Staple the zipper to the inside of the bag on both sides of the opening. Cover stapled seams with duct tape.

Step eight:

Run an extra piece of tape along the zipper seams to connect the two sides. This will finish the top edge of your bag.

All Tied Up

Neckties aren't just for business. Use an old tie to create an unforgettable evening bag. Carry this purse to the mall, a party, or to a formal event. Look in thrift stores or family members' closets for the longest and widest tie you can find.

You Will Need:

necktie
measuring tape
needle and thread
scissors
small piece of Velcro
chain
embellishments

Sewing by Hand: Slide the thread through the eye of the needle. Tie the end of the thread into a knot. Poke the needle through the underside of the fabric. Pull the thread through the fabric to knotted end. Poke your needle back through the fabric and up again to make a stitch.

Continue weaving the needle in and out of the fabric, making small stitches in a straight line. When you are finished sewing, make a loose stitch. Thread the needle through the loop and pull tight. Cut off remaining thread.

 Step one:
Find the narrow end of the tie. Make a fold 5 inches from the end of the tie.

Step two:

Starting at the fold, sew the bottom edges of the tie together.

Step three:

Fold the edge of the tie over. The seams will slant upward. The tie will also spiral upward. Sew the bottom of the long part of the tie to the top of the folded section.

Tip: Be careful to sew through only one layer of the tie. If you sew both layers, you'll sew the bag shut.

Step four:

Continue sewing until you are 6 inches from the end of the tie. Knot and cut the thread.

Step five:

Fold the wide end of the tie flat against the top of the bag. The tip of the tie will stick out to the side.

continue on next page

Step six:

Sew Velcro to the flap and the bag.

Step seven:

Sew the chain to the tie.

Step eight:

Add embellishments.

Tip: For a wide, short bag, make your fold 8 or 10 inches from the narrow end.

Push the Envelope

Send a stylish message with this easy envelope clutch. Dress up this simple craft with a swatch of fun fabric and some snappy buttons. Use trendy prints or bright colors, and with a few folds, you'll be carrying a piece of your very own runway art.

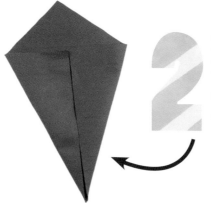

You Will Need:

14 square inches of
    stiff fabric such as
    ultrasuede, vinyl,
    or oilcloth
two clothespins
needle and thread

scissors
two small buttons
one large button
pencil
hole punch
self-adhesive
    embellishments

Step one:
Lay the fabric square on your work surface, like a diamond.

Step two:
Fold in the side corners toward the center on a diagonal. Your fabric should be in a long kite shape.

swatch—a small piece of fabric

continue on next page

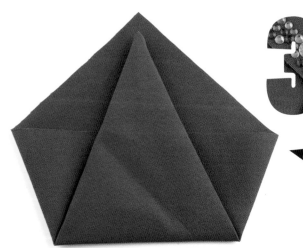

Step three:

Fold the bottom corner up toward the top corner. The bottom point should be 1 inch below the top corner.

Step four:

Fold the bottom point over the center flap. Secure the corners with the clothespins.

Step five:

Sew the small buttons where the bottom corner folds over the side. Be sure to only sew the top layer of the purse. Cut and knot the thread. See sewing instructions on page 16.

corner

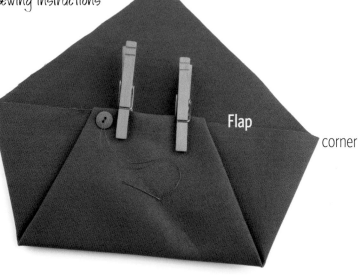

Flap

corner

Step six:

Sew the large button onto the bag about 2 inches from the bottom. Cut and knot the thread.

Step seven:

You'll need a buttonhole to close your purse. Fold the top corner of the purse over the bottom and side corners. Lightly mark where the button touches the top flap of your purse.

Step eight:

Using the hole punch, punch two holes at the point you marked. They should be about as close together as the width of your button. Cut a line between the holes to make a buttonhole.

Step nine:

Add embellishments.

Add a Little Zip

Who says you have to choose between being pretty and being strong? Flowers made from metal zippers can be both. With hundreds of colors to choose from, these zipper flowers have just the right amount of sparkle.

You Will Need:

zippers with big metal teeth
scissors
needle and thread to
   match the zipper tape
hot glue
an old handbag

Step one:
Unzip zippers
so you have two
separate pieces.

Step two:
Cut ends off zippers and
remove metal pull tabs.

 ## Step three:

Fold zipper onto itself to create petals. Stitch through the zipper fabric to anchor the petals. Repeat until most of the zipper is used.

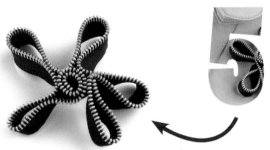

 ## Step four:

When you reach the last couple inches of the zipper, tie the thread off and cut it.

 ## Step five:

Tightly roll the end of the zipper. Use the needle and thread to make a stitch every few rolls. This will keep the zipper together.

 ## Step six:

Push the roll into the center of the flower. Stitch the roll to hold it in place.

Step seven:

Hot glue flowers onto handbag. Make sure to glue both the center of the flower and the petals.

Tip: If hot glue isn't strong enough, you can sew the flower onto the purse with a heavy-duty needle and thread. Use a thimble to help push the needle.

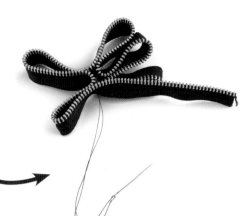

Sweet Paint Job

Give this bag a custom feel with a simple paint job. The bag's colors and your monogram will show people the real you. Take a preppy green bag to school or choose black for a more posh look. White goes anywhere, and metallic tones will get you noticed for sure!

You Will Need:

- large mailing sticker
- canvas tote bag
- masking tape
- paintbrush
- acrylic or fabric paints in three different colors
- pencil

Step one:

Place mailing sticker in the top center front of the bag. Press down firmly.

Step two:

Lay masking tape diagonally along the front and back of the tote, leaving equally sized stripes in between. Press down firmly on all of the tape.

Step three:

Paint the exposed parts of the bag with one color of fabric paint. Be careful not to let any paint soak through the masking tape. Let bag dry.

monogram—a decorative symbol usually made up of a person's initials

tone—a shade of color

Step four:

Tape off the edges of the bag by the handles. Paint the handles with the second paint color. You may need to let one side dry before painting the other side.

Step five:

After the paint has dried, remove the tape and sticker.

Step six:

Lightly draw your letter of choice in the rectangle left behind by the mailing sticker.

Step seven:

Paint your monogram in your chosen color. Let dry.

Step eight:

Use your third paint color to add polka dots around the rectangle. Or make dots or narrow pinstripes in between the painted stripes.

Sticky Style

Duct tape bags and wallets have been spotted in stores and on the runway. But plain old silver is too blah for the stylish fashionista. Pump up the girl power with a bold pattern, bright colors, and a little bling to finish things off. Carry your purse to lunch with your best buds, and bet them dessert that they can't guess what it's made of.

You Will Need:

scissors

measuring tape

two rolls of duct tape in different colors

self-adhesive Velcro dots

Step one:

Cut a 20-inch long piece of tape in your main color. Lay the tape horizontally on a table. Fold the bottom edge up to meet the top and press to seal. Make eight of these.

Step two:

Cut an 8-inch long piece of tape in your second color. Fold into a strip as in step 1. Make 20 of these.

Step three:

Cut an 8-inch strip of your first color. Lay it on your table sticky side up. Place the long strips side by side on the top half of the tape.

Step four:

Slide a short strip of tape under the first long strip. Continue weaving the strip through the long strips.

Step five:

For the next strip, alternate the weave (over then under). Keep weaving the short strips into the long strips. Always alternate the weave for each strip.

Step six:

Lay an 8-inch piece of any color tape on your work surface. Press the tops of the long strips onto the bottom half of the tape.

Step seven:

Lay strips of your main color tape over your weaving, sticky side down. Be careful not to lay tape over the top and bottom pieces of half-covered tape. Overlap the strips a bit so there are no gaps. Fold the top and bottom edges over.

continue on next page

Step eight:

To make side panels for your purse, cut two 6-inch pieces of tape. Lay them down sticky side up, overlapping by ¼ inch.

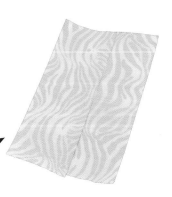

Step nine:

Lay a 7-inch piece of tape, sticky side down, on the two overlapping pieces. Repeat steps 8 and 9 to make the other side panel.

Step ten:

Starting at the front corner, press the side panels against sides of the woven mat.

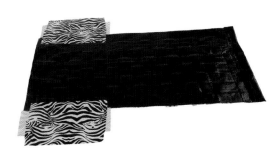

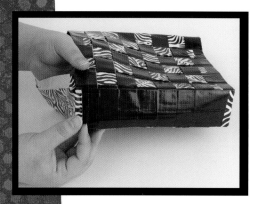

Step eleven:

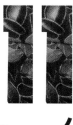

Attach the bottom of the side panels to the underside of the mat. Fold the mat the width of the side panel to make the bottom of the purse. Tape the bottom of the purse.

Tip: One 15-yard roll of duct tape in each color should be enough to make two purses. So make a matching purse for your BFF!

Step twelve:

Fold the top tabs on the side panels down into the inside of the bag.

Step thirteen:

Attach the back edges of both side panels to the mat.

Step fourteen:

Tape the inside of the bag where the edges meet. Tape around all seams and outside edges of the bag.

Step fifteen:

Cut a 24-inch piece of tape in your main color. Fold the edges together like in step 1. Tape one end of the strip to the inside of the bag on each of the sides.

Step sixteen:

Stick a piece of Velcro to the underside of the flap and to the bag where you want the flap to attach.

Glossary

decoupage (day-koo-PAHZH)—a liquid glue used in craft projects

envy (EN-vee)—to want something owned by another

grommet (grom-MET)—a loop that strengthens or protects an opening

monogram (MONO-gram)—a symbol of identity, usually someone's initial or initials

sentimental (SEN-tuh-men-tuhl)—resulting from feelings rather than facts

swatch (SWAHTCH)—a small sample of fabric

tone (TOHN)—a shade of a color

Read **More**

Civardi, Anne. *Bags and Purses*. World of Design. Mankato, Minn.: Sea-to-Sea, 2010.

D'Cruz, Anna-Marie. *Make Your Own Purses and Bags*. Do it Yourself Projects! New York: PowerKids Press, 2009.

Link, Mary. *Fast Fun & Easy Fabric Critter Bags: From Stuff Stashers to Beach Bags to Pillowcases.* Lafayette, Cali.: C&T Pub., 2007.

Internet Sites

FactHound offers a safe, fun way to find Internet sites related to this book. All of the sites on FactHound have been researched by our staff.

Here's all you do:

Visit www.facthound.com

Type in this code: 9781429665506

Super-cool stuff! Check out projects, games and lots more at
www.capstonekids.com

Index